Boston Pub
Boston, M

TANTALUS
IN LOVE

Poetry

After the Digging

The Courtesy

Happy Hour

Covenant

Mixed Company

Selected Poems, 1974–1996

The Dead Alive and Busy

Song and Dance

Prose

In Praise of the Impure:
Poetry and the Ethical Imagination

The Last Happy Occasion

Vigil

Translation

The Oresteia by Aeschylus

ALAN SHAPIRO

TANTALUS IN LOVE

Houghton Mifflin Company

BOSTON   NEW YORK

2005

For information about permission to reproduce selections from this book, write to Permissions, Houghton Mifflin Company, 215 Park Avenue South, New York, New York 10003.

Visit our Web site: www.houghtonmifflinbooks.com.

Library of Congress Cataloging-in-Publication Data

Shapiro, Alan.
Tantalus in love / Alan Shapiro.
p. cm.
ISBN 0-618-45242-7
1. Love poetry, American. 2. Divorce—Poetry. I. Title.
PS3569.H338T36 2005
811'.54—dc22   2004059441

Book design by Anne Chalmers
Typeface: Perpetua

Printed in the United States of America

MP 10 9 8 7 6 5 4 3 2 1

Grateful acknowledgment is made to the following publications, in which these poems originally appeared: *Agni Review:* "Lament," "Premonition." *At Length:* "Tantalus in Love." *The Forward:* "Instruction." *Kenyon Review:* "Take Off," "Ghost Watch," "The Haunting." *Rivendell:* "Lookout." *Slate:* "Iris," "That and This." *Threepenny Review:* "Space Dog." *TriQuarterly:* "Medley," "Anger," "Lily Pond." *Virginia Quarterly Review:* "Super Bowl Party," "The Conversation."

"Lament," "Iris," "Protest," "Yes and No," "Sunflower," and "Actaeon and Diana" were inspired by Frank Hunter's incredible photographs. For help with these poems, I want to thank Joseph Regal, Tom Sleigh, David Ferry, C. K. Williams, Robert Pinsky, Reginald Gibbons, Jason Sommer, Daniel Wallace, John Rosenthal, Michael Collier, Richard Bausch, and Allan Gurganus.

For Callie, E. F. forever

CONTENTS

INVOCATION

Days pass and years vanish, and we sleep-
    walk blind
among miracles. Love, fill our eyes
    all up with seeing!

Let there be never again
    a moment in which
your sudden shining isn't
    sudden as it rends

the dark we walk in. Make us see
    no matter where
we gaze that the bush burns
    unconsumed.

And we, the spun clay, will rise
    to a receding
holiness and sing, as it recedes,
    How filled with awe

this place is, and we did not know it.

I

TANTALUS IN LOVE

1

The trees let down
their branches to his out-
stretched hands,
                    lower
and still lower,
                    the branches
bending like a taut
bow from the weight of fruit
that flashes
                    everywhere
among the leaves, right there
beyond his fingers, at
his fingers, the dazzling
lusciousness
                    brushing
his fingertips so faintly
that there isn't any
difference
                    now between
a promised touch
                    and touch.

Are you? Is there someone?

The camera inside his head
doesn't want to get

involved,
> will not take sides;
from high above them,
> coolly
it pans away from him,
back curved like a question mark,
elbows on the table,
hands holding up his chin,
to her,
> the very image
of resistance, deflection,
steely withdrawal as,
her chair pushed back, legs crossed,
arms folded on her chest,
her face not facing his,
she's looking out now through
the window at something that
he can't quite see from where
he's sitting,
> unreadable,
but asking to be read —
> as if
the fruit were reaching down
for him to feel it, take
it, hold it in his trembling
hand

How do you explain

though every time his hand strains
higher for it

       What
the hell does this mean

it only springs back
higher up the branch

That's none of your

And don't you ever again

and all he has is air,
the prickling leaves,
               her face
averted,

           What do you want
from me?

            a fragrance grown
so thick around him that
it's nearly visible,
a sweet vaporous twining
up and down his skin,
along his nose,
             across
his parched, still opening mouth

2

The nearness of it, the right
there too bright mocking
plenitude that leaps away
so teasingly each time
he grabs for it that every
time he can't help think
this time he nearly got it,
he came so close, and so
he's even hungrier,
more eager than before
to try again —

                          "Do you
still find me attractive?"

She doesn't turn her head,
and as he waits, the camera
entertains him with
some recent clips
of how she lately,
whenever he goes to kiss her,
turns her face away
as if to fend him off
by offering the cheek
only, never the lips,
deigning
            (that's how it feels)
to let him kiss her there.
"So, do you?"

"Do I what?"
"Find me attractive?"
She sighs,
and the scent of all he craves
woos him no matter where
he looks —
"What kind of question
is that?"
"A simple one.
Are you attracted to me?"
"We've been married twenty years."
"Is that a yes or no?"
The lens widens to include
the late sun in the shot,
how it's angling down
through trees through the window
to her shoulder, arm, and hand
all speckled over now
with bits of light and shade,
light quivering with shade
and shade with light,
all swarming
in the agitated way
that cells swarm under
a microscope.
"I'm not
going to answer that."
"Why?"
"If you have to ask,
you wouldn't understand

the answer anyway."
"But I don't understand—"
"My point exactly."
"—why you can't just tell me
yes or no?"
                    "What if
my answer's no?"
                              "Is it?"
"This feels so coercive."
"It's a simple question,
yes or no."
                    "No."
"No?"
          "No,
it isn't a simple question."

          3

What *does* he want from her?
He knows what he knows.
                              He doesn't
need her denial
                    which
he wouldn't believe,
                              or her
confession
                    which she wouldn't give,
or might
                    but in a way
he knows
                    would make it all

his fault.
                    So why ask?
                                        He knows
what he knows.
                              He clenches
his baffled hands, turns
his head away from the coy
glitter of the dangling fruit,
shutting his mouth against it,
tightening his lips:
                              if he
could only seal himself
all up;
                    if only the camera
would just stop playing back
even the slightest of
their daily, nightly scenes:
the narrow bathroom,
                                        she
half dressed or naked
before her mirror, combing
her hair, or maybe trying on
some new shirt or blouse
                                        while he
moves past her, going to
or from the shower, unable
not
          to watch her,
                                        not
to brush her hip or thigh,
though as he does so
                              what

the camera shows is how
she just ignores it —

                              no,
"ignores" suggests too much
awareness —
                    how
                              she doesn't
so much as realize
he's there — his nakedness
invisible to her,
the restless ghost of a
desire neither mourned
nor buried,
                       so that now
the whole grove, each branch
of every tree, slips even
closer down around him,
soft as a loose gown,
                            and he knows,
were he to ask the camera
if there is dignity
in knowing
                    what he knows,
all it would give back
                        in answer
is
      the daily, nightly way
she never looks at him.

4

What about the water?
Wasn't he also standing
in water? Fresh water,
calm water, deep green yet
clear,
         you could see through it
all the way down to the bottom.

The camera doesn't care
about his new "discoveries,"
isn't impressed with his
for one thing
                  and another,
or how,
         when she said she was a
private person, couldn't
he understand that?
                  accept
that about her? she
just wanted her privacy,
he bit back, "No,
you're a secretive person,
there's a difference,"
                  a distinction
lost on the camera as
it just—
         cool water that
infuriates the thirst

which roars a firestorm
inside him,

          fire the very
coolness stokes —

             keeps moving
steadily toward her face
that won't turn, won't speak, fixed
on something out in the yard
the camera's scanning now,
showing
        whatever it is
she's looking at without
showing what it is . . .

5

But now he cups the water,
and this time it doesn't trickle
down
        between his fingers as
he lifts it,
          lifts it and sees
the gold fruit
           floating on
its surface, sees the water
and gold fruit cupped in his hands,
cupped and lifted to his lips,
lifted as thirst and hunger
blur to a single yearning

for the watery fruit
and fruit-like water which,
when he eats,

   when he drinks,
is a long shot

   of her walking
up the stairs,

  a man
behind her, his hands on her hips,
her hands on his,

   in perfect
step they slowly climb
the stairs together, the camera
following far enough
behind to take them both in,
all the way down the hall
into the bedroom

   where
it jump-cuts to the shadowy
rush of shed clothes,
the nearly indistinguishable
bodies on the bed,
the close-up of her face,
her eyes half closed,

   then closed,
lips open,

  moaning now,
now silent,

  still,

   shut tight

with what the camera
reveals
      as pleasure
so unambiguous,
complete,
         extreme,
               there's no
way to distinguish it
from pain, or punishment.

LILY POND

The water lilies floated
heavily in place,
like a lush mat
covering the pond
from end to end, the flat
leaves and giant pctals
all so still there
in that Medusa calm
that only the shrill whites
and blues and yellows
seemed to move, to
shimmer steam-like
in the heat haze.

To stand there at the edge
was to be breathed in
by the hot smell
of the flowering, inhaled
and held within
the microscopic
seethings and collapses
which I couldn't help
but feel were how
the flowers fed,
the very brightness
feeding on the eyes
that saw it, eyes that

couldn't look away,
consumed with looking —
what was it they were
looking for if not
for you, love, you
who were always
on the other side
of water, immersed
in shadows, in the cool
suspension of the only
element you must have
ever really touched
yourself within —

touching yourself,
I think now, how
could I not,
love? under
the hungry covers,
in all the ways
that you could never
say with me
you wanted, the secrecy
itself a flowering
of such intense
desire that it made
a room around you

(like the bedroom
we no longer shared)
and around the room

a house beside
a field at the farthest
edge of which
the speck of someone,
nobody you know,
is frozen stock-still
by the lily pond that
flares through those last
days with the very
heat that it deflects.

ANGER

One morning toward the end of twenty years
of marriage he awakens before she does
and watches her beside him, her back to him,
the covers pulled up tight and clutched in both hands,
her eyes tense, everything about her stiffened
even in dream against him, sealed away.
Unusual for him to wake before her.
Most mornings he's lulled from sleep in the half dark
by the low murmuring rivulet of words
the yoga teacher on the video
is speaking, and by the music that isn't music
so much as birdsong on the verge of music,
or music birdsong, some dreamy confluence
of one into the other, and she is there
in the TV's soft light, at the foot of the bed,
in pajama bottoms and a skimpy tank top,
her lovely body that he hasn't touched
in how long now? five months maybe? longer? the body
he knows he'll never touch again right there
before him, there to be looked at without her knowing,
being moved, it seems, yes, carried, drifted from pose
to pose by the whispery currents of the teacher's
urging — the Warrior, the Dog, the Dolphin,
and then the two he always waits for, the Cobra
that has her hips flat on the floor, arms pushing
up slowly, straightening while the back arches,
keeps arching till the breasts push out against

the tank top and the nipples show, and then
the one the Cobra mutates into, hands reaching
back behind her, holding her feet and pulling,
pulling her body up into the Bow
he almost thinks invisible hands are holding,
the expert fingers pulling the string back farther,
the unseen arrow poised, aimed, ready to fly—

Something in the undeniable failure
of who they are and have become together
allows him now, this morning, here at least,
if nowhere else, to think of what he did
or might have done to drive her off. Oh, he knows
he has his reasons for his anger, he is never
at a loss for reasons for his anger:
his sister's death, and then his brother's, and he
the youngest child, the baby, the last one you'd
expect to carry out the task, as in an old tale,
suddenly become the good brother,
the steadfast brother, there by the bedside,
right through their illness to their final breath,
the care itself the opposite of skill,
the kind of thing you do less well the more
you do it, and while he did it, needing her,
his wife, to somehow make it better, make
it all right, somebody for god's sake please
take care of the caretaker.
                              In the midst
of these calamities, how often would
he tell himself all bets are off? This is his time
to slam doors and belittle and still be loved,

never to have to bother with her terrors,
her needs. His time for once. Just his alone.
How could she stand it, really? What did she feel,
seeing him each day make his airtight case
against the world, proving again all through
his brother's dying what he had proved in
no uncertain terms throughout his sister's,
that there was never enough that anyone
could do for him, especially his wife?
Hadn't he proved this, so he could hate her for it?

One night not long ago, the children asleep,
they got to arguing over something, he can't
remember what, she was trying to explain
something to him, defend herself against
some accusation in his tone, which he
denied was there, and she insisted she heard,
when all at once he stood and grabbed a chair
and slammed it down and shattered it to pieces.
She was terrified, and he apologized,
then wanted to make love, it had been so long,
and she said, How can I touch you when you're like this?
And he snapped back, Well, maybe if you did
touch me I wouldn't *be* like this.

Sometimes
he almost thinks he's willed these losses, wooed them,
that they were sent to him as answered prayers.
No selfishness, no self-absorption, no
amount of treachery could ever sate
his appetite to be betrayed, neglected,

shunted aside, so he could feel himself
the righteously aggrieved, abandoned husband.
Wouldn't it be beyond his wildest dreams
if she were really having an affair,
as he accused her of having almost daily?
Who is it? Just tell me who it is. Is it
the yoga teacher, the chiropractor? Who?
How could she stand it except by pulling back
in self-protection and in doing so
play right into his hands and make him feel
so innocent, so noble, so deserving?

One night, a few weeks back, their anger spent,
exhausted into a rare intimacy,
an almost elegiac closeness, as if
they were remembering themselves like this,
being a couple, lovers, talking in bed,
she was telling him about this vision
she'd had while doing yoga, of this white light,
this warm miraculous white light that filled her
with inexplicable well-being. The vision
was all her own, it seemed, and no one's. Deep
within the self and yet completely separate.
A vision, she said, of being beyond the self,
even beyond life. Imperturbable,
Immovable. Eternal. Perfect and whole.

He notices how tightly his own hands now
are twisted in the sheets. He unshackles them.
As he slips from the bed, she stretches out,
relaxing now into untroubled sleep.

At the foot of the bed, he sees her yoga mat,
a darker shadow in the dark room.
And beyond the mat he sees the dormer window
where a few stars still quiver in the black sky.
Those stars will have already disappeared,
fading as the dawn sky brightens when
she herself lies down on the mat, on her stomach,
her back arching so slowly up into
the Cobra that it will look as if it's being
formed not by the pushing of her arms
but by some higher power, drawing her up.
That power will hold her in that pose a moment,
neck thrown back, her lovely neck, her face
looking straight up at the ceiling, before
it eases her back down, and with her forehead
on the floor, knees bent, hands behind her,
gripping her feet, it gently pulls her up
into the Bow.
                    What is it like to be held
that way, to hold yourself, so poised, so still?
As if you could be all one thing, complete,
enclosed.
                    Didn't someone say somewhere
that everything can be divided into
smaller and smaller pieces, that there is no
end to division, that infinity
extends down to the infinitely small
as well as up to the infinitely large?
So if you shot an arrow it would never
reach its target, since the distance could
be halved, and halved, and halved, ad infinitum?

He stands on the mat. Slowly, as if it were
a pose that she herself might do, as if
he too were being moved by something, he
turns sideways, toward the window, his gaze fixed
on a single star whose faint light makes the black
sky all around it even blacker; he raises
his arms until his right's extended straight
out toward the star, his left bent at the elbow,
two fingers pulling the string back farther and farther,
aiming into the darkness till he lets it go.

TAKEOFF

We didn't fall out of love,
old love, we rose — we rose
as in a plane, as in the moment
when the wheels lift
and the whole craft
shudders against the gravity
it then forgets as
all at once the runway's
fretful rushing by the window
slows and resolves to field
and tree line, the beaten
metal of a pond
the sun anneals;

we rose the way it all
grows clearer
as it diminishes till
a car drives in place
along a road that winds
and straightens, straightens to wind
again across a widening
landscape in which
nothing at all is moving
except the ever-
smaller sharper
shadow of our
getting clear of it.

THE HAUNTING

It may not be
the ghostly ballet
of our avoidances
that they'll remember,
nor the long sulks
of those last months,
nor the voices
chilly with all
the anger we
were careful mostly
not to show
in front of them,
nor anything
at all that made
our choice to live
apart seem to us
both not only
unavoidable
but good, but just.

No, what I think
will haunt them is
precisely what
we've chosen to
forget: those too
infrequent (though
even toward

the end still
possible) moments
when, the children
upstairs, the dinner
cooking, one of us
would all at once
start humming an old
tune and we'd dance,
as if we did
so always, in
a swoon of gliding
all through the house,
across the kitchen,

down the hall
and back, we'd sway
together, we'd twirl,
we'd dip and cha-
cha and the children
would hear us and
be helpless not
to come running
down to burrow
in between us,
into the center
of the dance that now,
I think, will haunt them
for the very joy
itself, for joy
that was for them,
for all of us

together, something
better than joy,
and yet for you
and me, ourselves,
alone, apart,
still not enough.

SPACE DOG

I did not know
that no one was planning
to bring me back, either.

— from "Laika" by Ben Florin

As if amazed it's his,
he holds his hand up
before the mirror, hand
too big now for the boy's
body, hand he's turning
slowly front to back
to front, then closes to
a fist he just as slowly
opens like an exotic
flower to its full extent.

The boy so newly merged
with the emerging man
it's hard to say what's boy
or man but for the eyes,
the boyish rapt confusion
in the look he looks
with at his mobile features
as he draws a blunt finger
over the shadow of hair
along his upper lip.

Shadow of hair in armpit,
crotch, voice deeper

than it was, then higher,
deeper, while the eyes
astounded, furtive, are the eyes
of someone who cannot
quite wake up from the dream
in which he suddenly
discovers he is naked
among a crowd of strangers —

or like the eyes of Laika,
Soviet space dog,
in an old drawing
I remember, the stunned,
not yet distrusting but
no longer trusting look
from within the comical
glass bubble of the gawky
helmet tilted atop
the comical white spacesuit,

as the spaceship hurtles
out toward the stars, the earth
a star behind it, the earnest
dog eyes fixed on black
space like a door
the masters have walked through
and will return from, surely.
Surely they'll come to get me.
Surely they didn't love me
all that time for this.

INSTRUCTION

My still wet daughter, unaware of me,
    after her bath,
the towel shawl-like on her shoulders,

has climbed up onto the chair
    she's dragged before
the mirror that's above the sink,

turning her body sideways, just to see.
    Her look is serious,
grim as a jeweler's before a rare,

ambiguously half-cut gem-
    stone even a slight
mis-tap would shatter. She looks severe

at first, perplexed, then almost troubled,
    like a student
with a problem she should get

but doesn't, or should have gotten
    sooner and is
stupider for having taken this

much time to get it, as she gets it now,
    or seems to, when
her fingers press the gorgeous belly

fat in farther than she can suck
        it in herself,
the exuberant belly, about which

I taught her once to sing "it must
        be jelly
'cause jam don't shake like that,"

now nearly diffident, on the verge
        of shame. O World,
meticulous instructor of the good looks

she soon will look for in mirrors all
        made merciless
by your instruction, what good does it do,

this father's two-bit wish to keep
        her safe from you
a little while longer? I

who despise you for your expertise,
        your avid skill,
yet know you as my mentor too,

I who have been your best, your least
        aware assistant
in all the places of your teaching,

who have stood where she stands now
        before your mirror,
imagining myself the man

the woman she's beginning to
           imagine might
imagine. She holds her breath to keep

the belly flat as she can get it
           before she breathes
out as herself again, and laughs,

turning to me, as if she's known
           that I've been here
watching all along and this

were all a show put on for my sake,
           a show she thinks
is over when I move to hug her

and she jumps down from the chair,
           slips from my arms,
away to a safe distance where

she almost seems to bow
           as she throws her dripping
hair before her and in a single

motion, straightening, ties the towel
           turban-style around it
just the way her mother taught her.

THAT AND THIS

There was that, and there was this.
There was that need for vindication,
there was this notion to forgive.

There was that pure amnesia
forgiveness insisted on, and there
was this insistence on the facts,

and then that enraged refusal not
to make a fine, that is to say
a just, that is to say exact

accounting of all the facts that made
it hard to sleep. Yes, there was still
that sleeplessness, and still the children's

lingering suspicion that divorce
must mean he was divorcing them,
since after all he was the one

who left. Still that, still this, and still
there was that night, past midnight, when
he noticed it was snowing hard

too early in the year for snow
and woke the children, and this way
their voices, thick with dream, kept asking

what? what? as he fumbled on their jackets,
and then that standing out in the street,
snow falling soundlessly about them,

snow that as he watched it falling was
one moment this or that single flake
that turned hypnotically in slow

and slower spirals, and then the next
was nothing but a rushing mass.
There was that too, and there was this too:

this walk to town, the children holding
his hand so tightly that he knew
they were a little bit afraid

and that his being out there with them
so late in snow and darkness made
the fear itself a keener pleasure.

There was the town entirely deserted,
the sidewalks gone in lunar drifts,
the street an incandescent whiteness,

and the traffic signals over the town's
three intersections dimmed to a gauzy
radiance, the colors merely colors

that signaled nothing, though they kept
on changing, flashing from that red
to green to yellow, trying, it seemed,

to recollect only enough
of what they used to mean to sharpen
this feeling of now forgetting it.

A PARTING GIFT

Songbirds are singing from a cave of leaves
inside a tree that I imagine there
beyond the upper-story window of
      the bedroom where
the lovers we no longer are
      are making love.

They're singing now because I say they do,
swallow and nightingale, wren, lark and thrush,
each song a different air of deepest pleasure
      all through a lush,
long night we'll never have again
      with one another,

a night of birdsong that won't let you sleep,
a night of hearing how each tremulous thread
of melody pulls back against the urge
      to pull ahead,
how song weaves in and out of song
      till all songs merge

into the sheerest billowing of air
that settles and never settles over all
the lovers do throughout that long-ago
      spectacular
lost night that's now forever my
      last gift to you.

II

HEARTH KEEPER

Long ago, there had been fire,
and they'd all gone into it,
my brother and sister,
                              a few
friends, too, and my parents
piecemeal.
                    And the fire
flooded up at first
                              like
brilliance from the wood,
                                        like
both a burning fount
called up
              by great thirst
and the thirst it quenched.

It raged, and then it didn't.
Then there was only
a lull of embers,
                          vague flares
like wakened absences
of fire dying down
to ash,
              and then ash-blunted
scrape of bronze
on stone,
                  a weight
of ash to lift,

and then the ash haze
left there in the shovel's wake.

How long have I been here
keeping the dark
                              in sight,
my mind the place in which
the dark's grown
conscious of itself as dark?

Come to me now, love.
                              I need you.
Come here.
                    How cold it's gotten.
Let my name in your voice be
the fresh disturbance,
the rippling
of char-scented air;
your touch the tinder.

AMARANT

Thir Crowns inwove with Amarant and Gold,
Immortal Amarant . . .

— Milton

Whose name holds
                    what contradicts
                                        its name,
unfading one,
                    un-
                              withering
                                        "fast by the Tree
of Life,"
              among the "Flowring
                                        Odours,"
                                                  never
not
        to be
                    the earliest
                                        diffusion
of itself
              as scent,
                    as ever-
                                        opening aureole
of petals that
                    are softer
                                        than the air
they open to,
                    soft
                              as the lover's lip

or tongue-tip

in a touch's

hesitant

first testing.

Flower less

of pleasure

than of the pleasure

pleasure

dreams of

in its late

returning,

returning as it has

to me

its longed-for

dream of dwelling

here

so far

inside this moment

of our moving

first

together that

the motion feels

like rest,

still life

in motion,

the very flower

flowering

on lip

and tongue,

as if

the name

alone,
                apart from what the name
                                  keeps locked
within it,
        safe
                between the letters
                              where it
can do no harm,
                were all the story was.

MEDLEY

A granite house. In the bedroom window a view
of the sea down a long spit. Brief gusts of rose
scent and salt scent slip through the billowy
come live with me and be my love white curtains where,
if we were listening, *melodious birds sing madrigals,*
and where, if we were looking, we could see
in flashes on the horizon how the low edge of the sun
has just now, *for thy delight,* brushed the wavery top
edge of its molten image in the water.

           A tongue of honey.
The bower of rough-hewn stones enclosing us
swirls in the very textures of its grain
the mineral remembrances of wayward winters, gales,
the scorching dog days, even as our bodies
move in a slow slide over and under, and through
the luffing curtains rose scent and salt scent,
had joys no date and age no need, wreathe
the invisible threads of their conditionals
so elusively about us that we still
believe they lead our lips, our tongues, our fingers
into places where we'll *all the pleasures prove.*

CAPE ANN

The day was all wind along the water,
great clouds massing and dispersing,
sun glare for a moment down the backs
of waves, then only gray waves breaking
against giant boulders in cascades
of salt spray that moistened the skin
and left it drier for the moistening.

We clambered over the granite slabs,
farther and farther from the town
till there was no one anywhere,
only here and there a lone
tern flying so low to the water
that we could see the wingtips
touch the whitecaps as it passed.

We wandered out there all that day,
our last good day together, though
I didn't know this then. I didn't
know the pleasure of the day
for you entirely depended
on your imagination of a future
you were certain even then

we'd never have. I didn't know
till long after it was over
that you needed an assurance

of other days as good as that
day was in order for that day
in all its goodness to mean
there should be more of them.

And since assurance like that wasn't
possible (how could it be?)
for us or anyone, the pleasure
you allowed yourself to take,
to yield to, was an "as if" only,
the day not even a day so much
as just the pretense of a day,

a kind of play that being play
enabled you to act as if
you were not acting, believable,
wholly there in character
of someone who was certain
of her own desire only within
the safety of that sly subjunctive.

You wandered off ahead of me,
looking for something, I didn't know what,
till you found a cave-like opening
in between two boulders
and climbed down into it.
By the time I reached you, you
had taken off your shirt, your shorts,

everything. Your body then
at just that moment a gorgeous

urgency of light and shade.
Hey, don't be shy, you called out
up to me above the boom
of water. Nobody can see us.
Don't leave me down here by myself.

LOOKOUT

Our lookout from the lighthouse on a cliff
        that shadows half
a granite quarry, half the water of it
a deep green calmer where a lone gull drifts,
        and half a sunlit foil.

Our lookout from that high room past the water
        past the white rocks
to the headland and beyond the headland out
where thunderclouds on top of thunderclouds
        on top of waves ride shoreward,

toward us, yes, but for now so far away
        the storm is just
the idea of a storm that lets the day,
lets that one day, continue as it is,
        unchanging as it changes

into the day that's now the underworld
        of every day
since then, my dreamscape, my desire's brooding ground,
the mischief of the two of us alone
        inside it, of it, safe

despite the sound of footsteps up the stairs,
        despite the faint
sound getting louder but still with floors and floors
to rise through, and on our fingertips, our lips,
        the scent of salt, the taste.

GHOST WATCH

The blood pooled in the fresh fosse
and up they drifted out of Erebus
like smoke from every side
in a listless swarming all around
Odysseus, crowding, pressing,
merging together, a cloud bank
of souls that swirled back as one
when he lifted his sword and then as one
surged even closer toward him
when he lowered it, their cries
unearthly, the very echoes of them
echoing for the blood drink
they would drink and know him
by and speak their recognitions.

But it was otherwise for us,
it was the blood surge and the rising
heat, the flurry and grasp and
cry of entering deeper into one
another that drove the ghosts off,
that harried them from us — dead
husband and ex-wife, and the lovers
before them, and before the lovers
even the gorgon shadow of parental
hovering — gone in the little
clearing that our passion made,
until we fell back, breathless, apart,

and they swarmed up out of hiding,
edging closer as the pulse died
down, and they were there beside us,
angry, wanting their own back now.

BOUNTY

Only the low whir of the blades
becoming louder as the fan
        turned toward us,
softer as it turned away;

only the faintest rippling
of cool air like a ghostly lotion
        that vanishes
as soon as spread along the skin

from shoulder down to hip, from hip
back up to shoulder, the sensation
        of it there
and not there, hardly felt so much

as sensed, not even sensed but dreamt of,
the very hair tips dreaming it,
        as you and I
adrift in one another dreamt

what we were doing as we did it,
adrift in fluencies that came
        as in a dream
unbidden, as in a lucky poem

whose turns are unpredictable
and just, our bodies easing out
      beyond the need
to ask, what will become of us?

no backwash of a memory,
no shifting weather but the fresh
      air that we could
and couldn't feel along the skin

that cooled and heated, heated and cooled,
all afternoon within the room
      in which we drifted
nowhere while the fan kept turning.

LAMENT

The look this child looks out with from
among the rose bushes and primroses
and other flowers not visible
enough to name is somehow bound
up with the way the dense thicket

of vines and leaf clusters have woven
all through and over the now mostly
hidden fence to frame the child's
face in a profusion of leaves
and blossoms — the look more beautiful

because it doesn't know it is,
because it holds now no expression
beyond this one of being held there
fast among the open-faced
frank petals in the early evening.

It is the same look I have seen
on your face, love, there in the just-
before of our intensest pleasure,
there as your face turns toward my face,
though not with gratitude exactly,

but just to show me with a child's
candor that you are there again,
for a moment, in the early evening,
among the leaves and flowers crossed
with shadows of leaves and flowers, there

where it's now only your own desire
for sleep that calls to you from the house
to come inside. I think the look
is asking how unthinkable it is
that you could ever not be happy.

DESERT WATER

for Callie

Is that it, love,
our last oasis
there where the very
air is shimmering
with the traces
of every other
place we had
to get to to
have gotten here,
each one a home
till only reached
or left, mirages
of belonging while
we were alone?

Is this it, love,
so long bereft,
we've had to teach
ourselves to make
oasis of
the in-between
where no place is,
not dwelling but
arriving ever,
thirsty, stumbling
near and nearer
till even the merest

opening
for touch becomes
a desert where
the dunes grow higher,
hotter, and
desire is distance
and distance water?

SUPER BOWL PARTY

Under the streetlamp
cars glistened end
to end clogging the cul-
de-sac and driveway
and even the front yard
of the small house whose
windows were shadowy
with friends you wanted me
to meet.
        And in the house
the game glowed from the big screen
and we in different phases
of our middle age
                milled
about it, drinks in hand,
watching, not watching,
drifting from small talk
to smaller talk, eyes
              shifting
from the
        changed formations, the
timing routes, the thud
of impact
        to whom-
ever it was we talked with
and then beyond them, slyly,
now and again,
           to others

in the room whose eyes were just
as slyly glancing at us
without appearing to.

The game glowed from another,
smaller screen in the bright
kitchen where Ann — your
dearest friend with MS
who'd broken up with Tim
the week before because
he drank too damn much
and she was sick of it —
was fixing him a drink.
   And where the beautiful
gaunt woman with high
cheekbones
      that were higher,
more beautiful for the gauntness,
the bald head,
      leaned against
her husband through the evening
under the blunt lighting
she must have surely felt
too looked at in,
      for hadn't
there been rumors of
a brief affair, his moving
out, then in again
when she got sick,
      so that
it almost seemed their every
gesture of affection

and solicitude,
                    which all
of us found so touching,
                              could
have been
              not only a late
imperiled flowering
of old devotion,
                    but
defiance too,
            of us,
of what they knew
                    we knew,
the very ones they charmed
all evening,
              leaning her head
against his chest, his hand
all evening on her shoulders.

The game glowed from the big screen,
the under-
              dogs were running
up the score,
              my eyes
were shifting from the adjustments,
the audibles, the cut-
back moves
              to you
in what phase of desire,
what entangling
                    shadows,

seeing for the first time
in years
          the ex who'd
cheated on you and
deceived you, and who now
was joking with the very
man you briefly
                    left him
for before his change
of heart that just as soon
as you returned
                    returned.

What
          shadowy hunger of
what understory
of relation on the
periphery
               of your
attention
               kept you silent
even when the streaker
streaked across the field
and held up play as someone
beside us muttered, "That's
as close to scoring as
we're gonna get"?
                    Thicket
of phases. Unspoken relations
of our middle age.
                    The game

glowed, nearly over.
                                We didn't
know Ann had disappeared
with Tim into the bedroom
till she, flushed and laughing,
in a silver and black dress
in honor of the losing
team, emerged
unsteadily, drink in one
hand, the other holding
on to Tim's sleeve.
                                And if
you wondered why she hadn't
warned you that your ex
would be there,
                        if
                                you thought
in her unhappiness
she might have grudged you this
new happiness with me,
                                despite
her love for you?
                        because of it?
you wouldn't say;
                        and I too
could not have told
                                the difference
then
        between affection and
a demonstration of
affection, affection as

defiance or revenge
or courtesy when in
full view
      of him you put
your arm around me, leaned
your head against my shoulder
and whooped
        and cheered more loudly
than the others as Ann,
          clinging
to Tim with one hand,
         drink
raised in the other to
the losing team,
        paraded
giddily from living
room to kitchen back
to living room
        in that
halting, brave,
        toddler half-
step way of hers that all
of us have lately noticed
getting so much worse.

ON HAVING TO STOP

The way it feels, there on the verge
of the first sip of the day's first drink,
the feeling that the moment this time
could be held, prolonged,

                    untouched
by both the itchy late-day yearning
for that first sip and the second sip's
already too

         much too late too
far gone fuck-it-ness; the way
the shot glass

           gold up to the rim
continues brimming even as
from lip to tongue to throat well-being
burns its golder promise of a life
so dense with possibility
that possibility's itself
achievement,

             that first sip both
the work and the reward for work,
both the performance and applause;
the way now on the anniversary
of Tim's death I see him on the night
we met, holding that shot glass up
and saying, This, boy, when you die
and go to heaven and God comes up

to you and puts his arm around you
and says, Welcome home, son,
                                    this,
you're gonna smell this on his breath.

PREMONITION

Two lovers talking on the phone at night,
ear pressed to the receiver pressed to ear

for the half-whispering voices that are clearer
for being quiet, more intimate

somehow for being far away. The timbre,
pitch, and exact inflection of who they are

in saying what they want, what they would do
if they were there together, has never been

so audible; as if the sheer voice stripped
of body were revealing something about

the nature of their love not just for bodies,
but of his body for hers, and hers for his,

the lovers never more exactly there
though less material, never more held,

more truly clung to than in separation —
I wish I could take you in my mouth right now —

I wish your lips were here — the voices hungry,
ghost-like, and won't it be like this one day,

only the voice returning to the stark bed,
voice rising up from where nobody rises,

your voice or mine, to haunt us as tonight
our voices haunt the hand that moves like the lips

that speak the words of what the lips would do?

ACTAEON AND DIANA

No place to look for, only to happen on.
Everywhere, the slender sound of rain
after the rain has stopped, a hearsay more
than sound of water you are helpless not
to follow all the way down the valley to
a hidden cavern over the high lip
of which the water changes as it spills
from mere water into incandescent mist
that brightens the dark surface of the pool
it falls into with even denser shinings.

The dark pool and the darker cave and even
the trees descending toward you from the white
light high above them in degrees of darkening
all grow darker down here for the shining.
No place to look for, no place ever
to expect to find and once you find it ever
to hope to dwell in or escape. The way
the mist hints at the hair the hunter caught
a glimpse of, the celestial flow of it
about the goddess as she let it fall

still bearing traces of the loosened braids,
the shining goddess gone as soon as seen,
the bright hair just the afterglow of hair
left in the air a moment above the pool
to dog the hunter no matter where he goes,

the hunter hunted by that vanishing
as you yourself will be for seeing this,
you too be scented out, pursued, as if
the punishment for such a pleasure were
the vision of it once the pleasure's gone.

III

IRIS

Love flower of the middle-aged,
the interanimating pain
and beauty in the way the stalk
bends under the unexpected weight
of the still uncrumpling gaudy tissue
of the newest blossom
                while
the lower blossoms like a ghostly
time lapse in reverse appear
to shrivel into themselves and turn
away forlorn before they fall,
the way the snapshot fell from its sleeve
into her lap,
              and there she was,
my new love with her old love years
before beside a lake with blue
hills in the distance rolling down
to bluer water, and there they were,
the lovers, naked, hand in hand,
both smiling back
              at me a smile
of joy so new so mischievous
you couldn't look at it and not
believe no lovers ever gave
themselves so freely to each other.
The flower bends under the blossom's

weight; it trembles, bending

                     it almost

seems

        to hold it up, as if
to hold it there forever, its one
and only darling, honey child,
how did I ever live without you?
How could I ever let you go?

PROTEST

for Annie Dillard

I can almost
hear the thudding
echo of each
apple as
it hit the grass
from how they now
lie scattered helter-
skelter all
around the tree.

I can see too
how the bruised
and mottled grass-
streaked rugged
spheres of apple
(like a child's drawing
of the planets), if
taken together,
seen as one,
resolve into
a single almost
luminous sphere
that is a kind
of echo of
the heavily over-
arching branches.

And in the branches,
among the sharp,
torn, curling
oblong leaves
whose moody sheens
dissolve into
the very darkness
they hold back,
there are no apples
fully visible
but one, one
isolated
radiant sphere.

Where are you now,
you ancient sleights
of solace, airy
balms that would
convince me that
the agony
of losing this
loved face, that never-
to-be-repeated
stumble of a
laugh, should
be less because
it is the living
tree that matters,
and not this one
soon-to-be-falling

apple whose very
shape is the shape
the mouth makes when
it's crying No?

YES AND NO

The last light
caught in the highest
branches seems
at this very moment
caught between
the black night
that has risen up
the bole of each tree
from the mineral dark
beneath us, and
the night the night
is pressing down
against us from
beyond the stars.

The last light is
less a light now
than a pale burning
from within and all
along the fine
reticulating
system of
the branches to
the tips of twigs
and last leaves and
beyond them as
smoky aura, the
whole structure

seeming at once
to blur and sharpen,
tense with desire
to go on being
what it is
at the very moment
that the desire
is overcome.

Like the last look
the dying give us,
the taut features
saying at one
and the same time
no not this, no
anything but
this, and yes, this,
this, at last.
                    Yes,
you can see
how the soul itself,
its loved and tortured
history,
            is caught between
the one night
and the other,
here in the branching
fire and the fire-
like branches
giving out
into the air.

SUNFLOWER

Ah sun-flower! weary of time
———Blake

No pitying
"Ah" for this one,
no weariness
about it or
wanting in the
upward heave
of its furred stalk
curving and opening
out into a
cup of pointy
leaves, each leaf
alert with tiny
quills, spines,
prickles—
         did I
say *cup*
     of leaves?
Say shield instead,
say living
crucible
from which flames
burst with such
sticky brightness
that they suck
sunlight down
into the in-

fluorescent burning
pit of itself.
                Did I
say sunflower? Say,
instead, don't-ever-
mess-with-me. Say
there-is-nothing-
I-won't-do-to-live.

THE CONVERSATION

Sun flickers through the trees beyond the window
outside the room in which we sit all morning,
talking around the table whose wooden surface
quickens with shuttled light and shade, leaf shadow
and sun both weaving and woven, each by each,
as if the table were remembering
within its grain the living tree it was.

All morning as we talk inside the room
around the table, our bodies are aswarm
with light and shade, our voices like a web
hung in the air between us, stitching and
unstitching in the telling and the hearing,
the taking issue with, concord and discord,
every one of us around the table

at one and the same time Penelope and suitor,
the wily mistress unraveling what she weaves,
and the brash lords impatient for an answer,
the unhemmed shroud itself a keeping faith,
a holding off of the tyrannical,
wealth-squandering, and inhospitable
insistence on a final yes or no.

Another time, around another table,
I listened to a woman scholar read
from an ancient story, a poem about a girl,

the sister of a queen, whom the king rapes,
cuts out her tongue so she can't tell her story,
locks her in a tower where she stays
until she weaves the story of what he did

into a gift of sorts, a fabric she has
delivered to the queen, who frees the girl.
And after vengeance more unspeakable,
they're all turned into birds whose very songs
wreathe the deceit and mutilation and
revenge into the cadence of the poem
the woman wove into a fresher version

of the ever-changing forms that bonds
of love and violations of those bonds
and appetite and greed assume
in their migrations from an ancient tongue
into the living voice, that woman's voice,
Ovid become the scholar reading him
to us inside a room around a table.

And as I listened I remembered a story
the father of a friend of mine told him
one night at dinner, around another table,
in a small kitchen in the Bronx, a story
the father's father told him as a last gift
on a cattle car, before the herding off
and the selection — the story itself a thread

torn from the fabric of a people, the whole
cloth of a people trampled and ripped and burned

away to ash except for this one story
my friend repeated to a few of us
twenty years later around another table,
his own voice twined with his father's as he told

the sacred story of a holy man
who when his people needed him for something
would go into a clearing in the woods
and light a fire, and there in the tangling light
and shade, with night birds singing from the trees
beyond the fire, would say a secret prayer,
and whatever needed doing would be done.

And how his son, a generation later,
when called on by the people for the help
his father gave, would go to the same place
in the same woods and say, "We cannot light
the fire but we know the prayer, and that
must be enough." And what he had to do
was done. And his son, too, in turn, would find

the clearing, and say, "We can no longer light
the fire, we can no longer say the prayer,
but we still know this place, and that suffices."
But later still, whenever the people called
on the next son for some important task,
all he could do was sit down at his table
and say, "We can no longer light the fire,

we can no longer say the prayer, we do
not know the place, but we can tell the story

around the table of how it all was done."
My friend's voice twined with his father's twined with mine
as I then told the story in response
to what the woman read, and as I spoke,
and someone else replied, and others turned

the talk this way and that, I noticed how
our hands made flickering bird shapes in the mesh
of sun and shadow all along the table,
and in the pauses of our weaving words,
among the slips and silences, I heard,
or thought I heard, beyond the room, birdsong
crossed with birdsong within a shroud of leaves.